# 10 GOAL STOPPERS AND HOW TO BREAK FREE FAST

EFT TAPPING, MATRIX REIMPRINTING, MATRIX GOALS REIMPRINTING

CARYL WESTMORE

10 Goal Stoppers
&
How to Break Free Fast
with
EFT Tapping
Matrix Reimprinting
&
Matrix Goals Reimprinting

Note that for simplicity this book follows American English – if you spot any spelling errors that offend you – please forgive – or contact me – via FB messages or email - to point out any glaring inconsistencies – I'd be most grateful.

**Disclaimer**

**Please note that EFT Tapping, Matrix Reimprinting and Matrix Goals Reimprinting are still considered to be in experimental stages. Caryl Westmore offers these techniques as a personal performance coach and intuitive healer. She is not a qualified medical professional. Please take full responsibility for your health.**

*To all my wonderful clients, friends,*
*family and Nick Westmore*

*Thanks, with all my heart, for playing your part to make my dreams and*
*goals manifest and come true*

*To **you my dear Reader**...may you tap into **your** special dreams and goals to*
*fulfill the*
*LIFE YOU LOVE.*

# ALSO BY CARYL WESTMORE

You Can Break Free Fast EFT Tapping Emotional Freedom Techniques – 3 Simple Steps to get Unstuck and Attract the Life you Love, Foreword Dr Joe Vitale

5 Steps to Goal Success EFT Tapping, Matrix Goals Reimprinting, Foreword Karl Dawson, EFT Master, Hay House author

Online Dating Success Secrets for Women 40/50+ How to find True Lasting Love – Attract your Love Hero, Dump the Love Villains, *Like I did!*

\* \* \*

# FREE GIFT

## WANT TO ATTAIN YOUR GOALS FASTER?

**MANIFEST YOUR DREAM LIFE FASTER**

**Create your Perfect Ideal Day (Heaven vs Hell)**

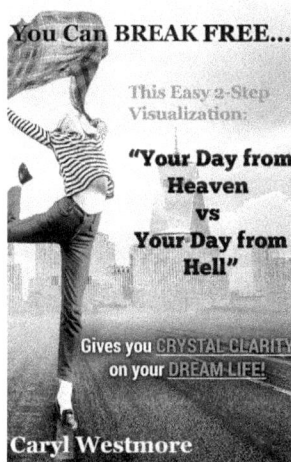

*Click on image to get this fabulous goal-setting Journal Exercise*

# INTRODUCTION

## THE PAIN OF "GOAL SHAME"

Do you suffer "goal shame" for failing to achieve goals that you know would make a huge difference to your life, income, health and happiness?

Are you fed up and frustrated because this past year you set out with high intentions – but failed to …

- Write your book
- Get more organized
- Make and save more money
- Lose weight and get fit
- Quit smoking/eating sugar/biting your nails
- Attract true soul mate love
- …………………………………………….fill in the blank

You're not alone. Each year GAZILLIONS of people discover that the fireworks of their New Year Resolutions simply fizzle out and die.

*They become crushed or aborted within days, weeks or a few months after January 1.*

Psychologist John Norcross with researchers at the University of Scranton in the USA found that **only 8% of people actually succeed with their New Year's goals.**

* * *

If your sacred dreams to write your book, blog or other creative project, lie withering in your heart – *like raisins in the sun or festering sores* – as poet Langston Hughes so vividly puts it, then you're in the right place.

If you really _really_ want to do something to bring your goals back to juicy life and make them happen in the coming months/year then you're in the right place.

Lurking like sharks somewhere in the deep waters of your mind you'll most likely find one or more of the 10 "goal stoppers" described in this book.

These goal stoppers are keeping you stuck and holding you back! As you read, intend that you will have an "aha" as you recognize any that apply to YOU right now.

My intention is that by the end of this book you will have discovered a truly cutting- edge revolutionary way to BREAK FREE from such blocks and to RE-WRITE and RE-VISION a success outcome for your dreams and goals.

**This is a list of the 10 MAJOR GOAL STOPPERS which I will cover in this book:**

- #1 Fear
- #2 Negative Beliefs
- #3 Poor self-image
- #4 Damaging Self-Talk
- #5 Bad Habits
- #6 A Single "Biggest Block"
- #7 Losing Momentum
- #8 Procrastination
- # 9 Perfectionism
- #10 Overwhelm

This book is a companion to: **5 Steps to Goal Success EFT Tapping, Matrix Goals Reimprinting** – Foreword Karl Dawson, EFT Master, Creator of Matrix Reimprinting.

There I explain a sure-fire method to set and get your "Golden Goals" or bucket list of dream desires that are part of your life purpose and the life you love. Both books together will make you unstoppable!

Dear Reader,

Below is a diagram of the Emotional Freedom Techniques (EFT) TAPPING POINTS.

At the end of each chapter you will find a blank **MY TAPPING POINTS** page where you can journal and note insights and AHAs you have about each goal stopper and how tapping reduces or changes it for you.

# WHO AM I?

**WHO AM I?**

My name is Caryl Westmore, Break-Free Fast Goal Success Coach, trained in The Journey, EFT Tapping and Matrix Reimprinting. I have a track record of over 20 years as an energy psychology and intuitive healing expert, coaching clients worldwide in person and on Skype and Zoom.

## MY SPECIALITY

**Matrix Goals Reimprinting is my speciality - helping people achieve their authentic heart-based dreams and goals by releasing the past and rewriting the future.**

Just like I did! Just like you can!

I hold nothing back in my EFT Tapping books about my own Cinderella story from "mess to success" achieving my dreams and goals.

I believe if I can do it...LIVING MY DREAM LIFE TODAY despite growing up in an alcoholic home in Zimbabwe, being stuck in a difficult 25-year marriage in South Africa and eventually reaching rock bottom after losing my dog and house in a fire... then so can YOU.

## DRAMATIC SHIFT

After the fire in 1999 my life shifted dramatically as I discovered the tools of emotional healing that include EFT Tapping, Matrix Reimprinting – and now Matrix Goals Reimprinting. I also became skilled at applying the Law of Attraction in important ways that actually worked!

## MY LIFE MISSION

As a result, my own life mission became a journey to help others as an intuitive "Break-Free Fast" coach and trainer. My books, all available on Amazon and Audible, reveal the magic way this exciting cutting edge approach can work to help YOU to break free! Rapidly!

* * *

# NEED HELP?

**CALL ME FOR HELP**

If at any time you feel you need my support or help – reach out to me for a paid session on Zoom or Skype. Get my special rate of $99 (instead of $200) for readers of this book only) to clear your feelings, fears or blocks to goal success.

In the email header put "Goal Stopper Session"
contactcwestmore@gmail.com

# THE EFT TAPPING POINTS

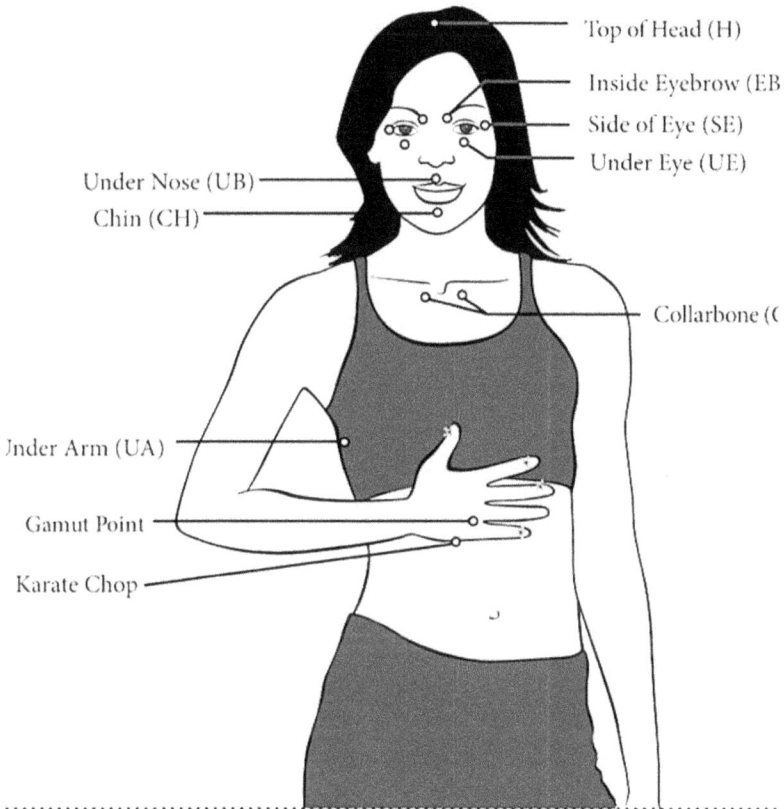

Top of Head (H)
Inside Eyebrow (EB
Side of Eye (SE)
Under Eye (UE)
Under Nose (UB)
Chin (CH)
Collarbone (C
Under Arm (UA)
Gamut Point
Karate Chop

| | |
|---|---|
| Top of head *(H)* | Inside Eyebrow *(EB)* |
| Side of Eye *(SE)* | Under Eye *(UE)* |
| Under Nose (UB) | Chin *(CH)* |
| Collarbone *(CB)* | Under Arm *(UA)* |

HAND: Thumb, Index Finger, Middle Finger, Little Finger, Karate Chop/Side of hand.

# Now let's explore which of the 10 Goal Stoppers could be holding YOU back!

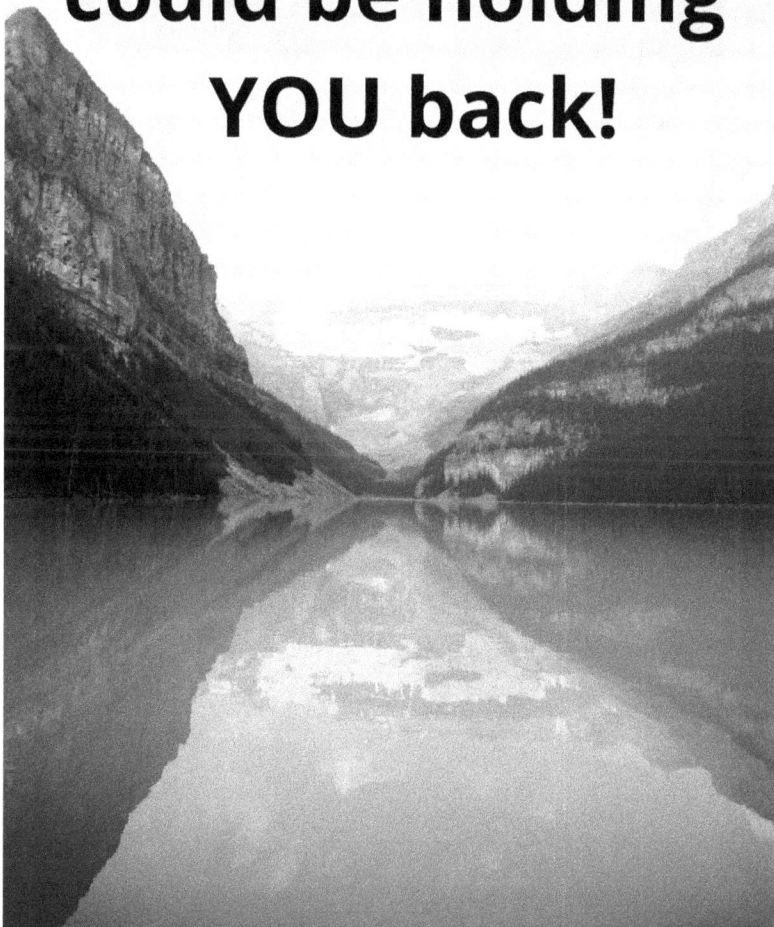

# CHAP 1 FEAR

*G*oals are about growing your life – and with growth comes FEAR.

**"Every time you take a step into the unknown, you experience fear,"** says Susan Jeffers, author of Feel the Fear and do it anyway.

> "There is no point in saying, 'When I am no longer afraid, then I will do it.' You'll be waiting for a long time. The fear is part of the package".

The package she refers to is our primitive cave-man brain - also known as the amygdala.

Fear is hard wired into our brains in the amygdala to protect us from danger and death - or the threat of pain. It also stops us repeating life threatening situations (or perceived ones). It's a survival mechanism from 50 000 years ago when our cave-man ancestors faced sabre toothed tigers and ferocious predators.

It sets up the fight, flight or freeze response and for a child usually the only option is FREEZE.

In a 2005 Gallup poll (U.S.A.), a national sample of adolescents between the ages of 13 and 15 were asked what they feared the most. Fear of failure came fourth after terrorist attacks, spiders and death.

\* \* \*

## MAIN GOAL-STOPPING FEARS

**Fear of failure** is definitely very high on the list of goal stoppers.

Others include:
- Fear of making a mistake and looking stupid
- Fear of success (threatening the status quo or making family members or friends jealous)
- Fear of being ridiculed
- Fear of losing money
- Fear of being lonely and unloved
- Fear of rejection

\* \* \*

FEAR CRIPPLES **the ability to do things like stand up in public to speak, fly by plane or write a book. In the extreme it can become a phobia.**

If you don't break free and overcome the obstacles that fears put in the way of your goals and dreams, then your dreams stand to *shrivel and die like raisins in the sun*, to quote from a poem by Langston Hughes.

## HOW TO BREAK FREE

Goal stopping fears often go back to childhood events, humiliations or memories.

You must remove the negative beliefs that resulted as a consequence of these fears.

The good news is that with energy healing tools EFT Tapping, Matrix Reimprinting and Matrix Goals Reimprinting you can release and repair the fear-based freeze, shock or trauma crippling your goals and give the brain and nervous system a message of strength and positivity as you reimprint the memory and then step into a vivid picture of a hugely successful **Future Self** who has already achieved the goals.

# TAPPING NOTES

## FEAR

WHAT IS MY CURRENT FEAR?

On a Scale of 1 – 10 how intense is it?


WHERE IN MY BODY IS IT?

Does it have a shape, color or feel?

***Do a Round of Tapping***
   Test the new level of intensity (1-10)

   Does a past memory - person, place or emotion - come to mind
   while I tap on this fear? Journal your notes below…


         * * *


END SESSION

**Always end by tapping in the positive empowering reminder
phrase:**

**"I choose to let this go...right now I am safe and whole to pursue my goal."**

## FUTURE SELF TAPPING

Look into the future and see yourself having succeeded in releasing this fear. Attune with this Future Self...feel how they feel...see how they see the world with unshakable confidence in themselves to overcome challenges and fear.

# CHAP 2 NEGATIVE BELIEFS

*Change your thoughts, beliefs, and pictures of reality in your energy field or "the matrix".*

Many people believe that they are victims of life and circumstances and that reality is fixed. Yet what quantum scientists and experts like Dr Joe Dispenza or cellular biologist Dr Bruce Lipton teach us is that we are participants in creating this reality!

"Your life is a printout of your beliefs," says Bruce Lipton.

Metaphysical teachers like James Allen and Abraham-Hicks say the same thing.

"The outer conditions of your life will always out-picture your inner beliefs," wrote James Allen.

***A belief is just a thought you keep thinking,*** according to Abraham Hicks (a group of non-physical teachers of the Law of Attraction). They teach that our reality is made up of these consistent thoughts and beliefs.

Where do negative disempowering beliefs come from? Mostly

they are instilled during intense or fearful moments in the first six years of life by parents, grandparents, siblings, teachers and society – and beyond that from ancestral patterns passed down through the generations.

Many believe they also leak through from past lives.

\* \* \*

## COMMON EXAMPLES

Common examples of negative beliefs I've encountered are:

• I'M NOT GOOD ENOUGH – I was the dumb one in the family...everyone said so
  • I'm not worth it – no one ever wants to hear what I say • I can't do it (lose weight) – our family are all big – it's in my genes to be fat
  • I am alone; no one loves me – because that's how it felt since my sister died when I was three
  • What if... something bad happens – it always does, just when I'm starting to feel secure
  In my book **5 Steps to Goal Success EFT Tapping and Matrix Goals Reimprinting**, I describe several case studies that prove how I helped clients to source the root cause of a negative belief and transform it with positive empowering results.

## JACK HELD HIMSELF BACK

One such example was my client Jack who felt like a business failure, comparing himself unfavorably to his older, highly successful brother.

As we tapped and talked on this issue, he had a "break-free aha" when he went back to a specific memory as a teenager.

He recalled that most evenings he and his older brother used to jog round their neighborhood with their father.

But one day his brother, frustrated by the slow pace of their father, suddenly took off like a greyhound. My client had made a split-second decision to stay behind for his father's sake. In other words – he had felt the right thing to do was to "**hold himself back**" – something he had continued to do in life and business.

This went back to ECHOs throughout his early childhood. He had set up a belief at a very young age that unlike his older brother, he needed to be the "good boy" to earn love in his family. But after his session he now knew winning in business and life WAS AVAILABLE to him – he was free to go full out for his success.

## YOUR FUTURE SELF

One powerful way to imprint this in your mindset and belief system is to actually step into the future and feel what it's like to be changed and empowered as your Future Successful Self.

Matrix Goals Reimprinting gives you the exciting option to step into your successful thriving **Future Self** and get the energy, emotions and important insights and advice from that Future Self.

This works amazingly to blast goal stopping **negative beliefs** and reimprint them with powerful new pictures of success and achievement to resonate in your energy field and reality with the Law of Attraction.

# TAPPING NOTES

## NEGATIVE BELIEF

WHAT IS MY BIGGEST NEGATIVE BELIEF?

*O*n a Scale of 1 – 10 how intense is it?

WHERE IN MY body is it?

DOES IT HAVE A SHAPE, texture, color or feel?

## DO A ROUND OF TAPPING

Be curious and wonder...does a past memory - person, place or emotion - come to mind while you tap on this belief?

This may be from parents, siblings, teachers, or other influencers in your early years. (Make notes here or in a Journal about what they said, did or implied to instill the goal-stopping negative beliefs).

TAP ON THE MEMORY/MEMORIES AND FINISH WITH
THE REMINDER PHRASE: *"I CHOOSE TO LET THIS GO."*

Affirm the **opposite** of what you have believed too long about yourself, write it down below and tap in the new empowering belief
every day!

\* \* \*

END SESSION

**Always end by tapping in the positive empowering reminder
phrase:**

 "**I choose to let this negative belief go...right now I am safe and
whole to pursue my goal.**"

FUTURE SELF TAPPING

Look into the future and see yourself having succeeded in releasing
this negative disempowering belief and the story you told yourself
about it. Attune with this Future Self...feel how they feel...see how
they see the world with unshakable confidence in themselves to
believe in themselves, worth and goal success.

# CHAP 3 SELF IMAGE

❧

## POOR SELF-IMAGE

*Y*our **Self-Image** – good or bad – affects your Goal-Image and chances of success.

Because if you cannot "see" yourself as the kind of person who...

- achieves the success goal you want...
- the dream body,
- job,
- money,
- love partner

...this poor self image cripples your chances almost 100%.

\* \* \*

CYNTHIA KERSEY, best-selling motivational author and founder and CEO of the Unstoppable Foundation –has said:

> *"Believe in yourself and there will come a day when others have no choice but to believe with you."*

The Unstoppable Foundation's mission is building schools in places like Uganda and Nepal...and ultimately to ensure that every child on the planet receives access to the life-long gift of education.

In a recent interview Kersey, who is a contributing editor of Success Magazine and a regular guest on the Oprah network, said:

*"I realize that real change begins with my own ability to expand my belief in myself, to expand my consciousness about what is possible."*

Why is it vital to transform your poor self-image which is likely running continuously in your subconscious?

Because even if by enormous self-discipline and staggering effort you do achieve certain goals like lose the weight, meet your ideal man, land your dream job - if you have not changed your poor self-image something will happen to sabotage your lasting success.

## MANY EXPERTS BELIEVE THAT YOUR SELF-IMAGE IS THE NUMBER ONE FACTOR DETERMINING FAILURE OR SUCCESS WITH YOUR GOALS.

You may not realize how powerfully the past has fixed the mental picture you have of yourself NOW. You have internalized the judgments or intense experiences that happened to you as a child or teenager – and it's the negative ones that block you from achieving your goals.

They include beliefs about your abilities and deficiencies and whether you are lovable, capable or even worthy of success.

**If as a child if you were often told: "You're useless, stupid or will never amount to anything," then you will most likely grow up with a poor self-image as the result of this continuous physical and mental programming.**

But in some cases, it can be simply that you had an older sibling say 18 months to 2 years older who could DO so many things better than you. Perhaps you heard your family praising him for things he was doing and you felt over-shadowed.

Deep inside you concluded "I'm not good enough to...read, tie my shoelaces, run as fast as him."

This story sets in as a stigma of **NOT GOOD ENOUGH** that runs in your subconscious for the rest of your life.

## HOW A NEGATIVE BELIEF SETS IN

If you were told: "Be nice. Don't be selfish, put others first," then you may hold yourself back when it comes to achieving success in life. Taken to extremes this is a subtler but equally damaging brain washing which can squelch your ability to shine with your dreams and goals for fear of upsetting or "out-shining" others.

## MAXWELL MALTX

**Maxwell Maltz,** a New York plastic surgeon and author of Psycho Cybernetics (1960) discovered this truth when many of his clients that he made look great on the outside, often still felt ugly on the inside.

He called the brain **a self-image guided missile** and taught that by combining words and imagery, the brain could change the direction of previous thoughts and beliefs.

Maltz recognized that, in addition to the reconstruction work he did with plastic surgery on the outside, the patient needed to have reconstruction work on the "inside," *on their self-image.*

This is exactly what I do practically with EFT Tapping, Matrix Reimprinting and Matrix Goals Reimprinting.

## GOOD NEWS

So, the good news is – you can break free from this goal stopper by revisiting the ECHO – Your Younger Self "in the matrix" and giving him or her a new perspective, resolution, forgiveness and a chance to reimprint a **new empowering self-image**.

Stepping into the Future Successful Self always "seals the deal" in this regard.

# TAPPING NOTES

## POOR SELF IMAGE

How is your self-image influenced by your family of origin?

Think of a specific memory and rate it on a Scale of 1 – 10 how intense is it?

Where in my body is it?

Does it have a shape, color or feel?

DO A ROUND OF TAPPING ON YOUR YOUNGER SELF AND ADULT SELF

Tap until the painful memory is lessened and forgive yourself for letting it influence you for so long.

\* \* \*

END SESSION

**Always end by tapping in the positive empowering reminder phrase:**

"I choose to let this go...right now I am safe and whole to pursue my goal."

## FUTURE SELF TAPPING

Look into the future and see your Future Self having succeeded in releasing your **poor self image and claiming a new empowering self image.**

Attune with this Future Self...feel how they feel...see how they step into life expecting the best for themselves.

# CHAP 4 SELF TALK

⌘

## DAMAGING SELF-TALK

*O*ne guaranteed way to transform your **self-image** is with **self-talk**.

Our thinking is the one thing we have control over literally every moment of every day.

By ***NOT*** taking control of our **self-talk**, we become victims of bad habits, poor attitudes, and negative opinions, many of which are in our unconscious and hidden from our awareness.

### WHAT IS DAMAGING SELF-TALK?

Damaging self-talk is the internal voice (or voices) inside your head that picks up on the worst aspects of a situation you are facing or how you are handling it...and then sets up a running commentary in "inner critic" mode.

You trip on the carpet and the voice says: *"Clumsy idiot"*

You're running late and the voice says: *"Late again...typical. This time you'll get fired!"*

You write an essay and the voice says: *"Don't get your hopes up for high marks – you're not the smart one in the family."*

The voice can even be really mean and nasty making a cutting remark like: *"You lazy bitch!"*

The destructive result of this damaging self-talk is that it rips your self confidence to shreds and scuppers your goal-setting resolve.

Sensitive artists and creatives have to be particularly wary of the inner critic destroying the joy and success they would otherwise take in expressing themselves in their work.

## WHAT TO DO ABOUT IT?

Listen carefully for the "tail-enders" or unbidden words that pop up during an EFT Tapping session on an issue connected to your goals.

Also pay attention whenever you can to the ongoing inner dialogue you have running inside your head. Whenever you catch yourself muttering put-downs say: *"STOP... Cancel Cancel..."* and repeat something nice and empowering.

It is often a shock to discover the voices are repeating things that care givers, parents, siblings and teachers habitually said during your childhood. You are now treating yourself as unkindly as they did while also destroying your chances of goal success.

## CHANGING YOUR SELF-IMAGE CAN CHANGE YOUR LIFE.

*"Changing your self-image begins with changing your self-talk,"* according to Dr Jim Will, a psychologist who made a career of studying the self talk of athletes and people in business and advising them on how to transform their self-talk for optimum results.

He says:

*"From the moment we wake up in the morning to the second we go to sleep at night, we are all thinking, daydreaming, wondering, worrying, and having conversations with our self, whether we realize it or not. And the harsh reality is that most people's self-talk is rather brutal.*

*"We are all conversing with ourselves at an incredibly fast rate of speed – perhaps 10 to 20 times faster than we can speak out loud. The average person*

*tops out around 500 words per minute. Our internal thinking, our self- talk, is often running many times faster than we can talk out loud."*

And the worst part - it is estimated that your self-talk is between 60 and 85 percent **negative**, where you think mostly about what YOU DON'T WANT in your world.

Often when we do EFT Tapping our self-talk reveals itself in the rounds of tapping and talking. From here we can get curious as to where this language, attitude to ourselves and words originated.

## JIM CAREY

Why not take the initiative and combine clearing work with AFFIR-MATIONS to build up your self-image for goal success just like zany Golden Globe film actor Jim Carey did? Once struggling to make it in Hollywood, he eventually became a bankable comedy star with a string of movie hits.

In an interview in MovieLine many years ago he revealed:

*"I've always believed in magic. When I wasn't doing anything in Hollywood, I'd go up every night to Mulholland Drive and look out at the city, stretch out my arms, and say, 'Everybody wants to work with me. I'm a really good actor. I have all kinds of great movie offers'.*

*"I'd just repeat these things over and over, literally convincing myself that I had a couple of movies lined up. I'd drive down the hill, ready to take the world on, going, 'Movie offers are out there for me, I just don't hear them yet'.*

*It was like total affirmations, antidotes to the stuff that stems from my family background."*

**With EFT Tapping and Matrix Goals Reimprinting you too can test, challenge and change your self-talk.** You can change some of the negative aspects of your thinking by challenging the irrational stuck record parts, replacing them with more reasonable, upbeat and supportive words and images.

# TAPPING NOTES

## DAMAGING SELF-TALK

Write down one negative phrase you repeatedly say to yourself.
How is your self-talk influenced by your family, schooling etc?

RATE IT

Think of a specific person or memory originating your self-talk and rate it on a Scale of 1 – 10 for intensity.

Where in my body is it?

Does it have a shape, color or feel?

**Do a round of Tapping on your ADULT SELF and on your YOUNGER SELF**
Choose a new mantra or phrase to counter-act the negative damaging one.
**My new SELF TALK MANTRA is:**

State this new empowering MANTRA or AFFIRMATION for **30 days**

## END SESSION

**Always end by tapping in the positive empowering reminder phrase:**

**"I choose to let go this bad self-talk ...right now I am safe and whole to pursue my goal."**

## FUTURE SELF TAPPING

Look into the future and see your Future Self having totally released all habits of speaking unkindly to herself. Instead watch how your Future Self says sweet, empowering and encouraging words to support and help you succeed. Even if you make mistakes, she validates you.

Attune with this Future Self...feel how they feel...see how they see the world with unshakable confidence and self-love words they whisper, and say out loud to you.

# CHAP 5 BAD HABITS

## BAD HABITS

*H*ere are time-wasting bad habits that can sabotage you
achieving your cherished dreams and goals:

• **Spending too much time on Facebook and Twitter – and other
related internet activities**

• **Shopping**

• **Bingeing on alcohol, sugar and junk food – then feeling too
tired to accomplish your tasks**

• **Chatting or texting on your mobile**

• **Watching television and binge-watching Netflix**

Matrix Habit Reimprinting using EFT tapping was developed by
Sasha Allenby to help people overcome ingrained habits and addic-
tions like smoking, drugs, alcohol, caffeine, chocolate or sugar. It is
also useful to help you develop new habits to achieve your goals.

The technique is in three parts. It involves

1. Clearing previous life traumas (possibly past-life)

2. Changing the images of yourself in your field as a user of the
substance or performer of the habitual bad behavior and then

3. Creating a new field for yourself in relation to the addictive
behavior. You can read more about Field Clearing in Chapter 11 of
*Matrix Reimprinting using EFT* by Karl Dawson and Sasha Allenby.

Sasha applied Field Clearing to change her bad habits regarding eating and exercise.

## ADDITIONAL PRACTICAL TIPS

Use the following additional tips to transform your bad habits into good habits:

1. **Stop feeding yourself lies** that you "deserve" that sugary treat or cigarette because it makes you happier.

That's pure nonsense. The fact is you will be happier when you achieve your goal to:

- Lose 30 lbs – and be healthier
- Write that book – and expand your biz and message
- Quit smoking – and live longer

2. **Love yourself** enough to stop harming and hurting your body.

Taking care of yourself is a form of self-love, and the sooner you start, the sooner you'll feel good about it.

3. **Take tiny steps.**

As proven by Stanford professor BJ Fogg you will succeed if you learn the art of taking what he calls TINY HABITS or baby steps until after 30 days a new habit is ingrained as a success habit.

4. **Know your why** – and keep that motivation front of mind when you are tempted to waver.

5. **Track your bad habit triggers in a notebook.** Every habit is triggered by some event. A smoker may find she smokes when under stress, after a meal or when drinking coffee. By keeping a record of these triggers, she can become mindful and eventually change the pattern or action that causes the feeling that she needs a cigarette.

6. **Make a "QUIT PLAN"** with a deadline and get a coach or accountability partner to support you becoming the NEW YOU

# TAPPING NOTES

## BAD HABITS

WHAT IS MY NUMBER #1 BAD HABIT I AM CHOOSING TO CHANGE?

Do a round of tapping noticing WHEN and WHY you do this bad habit – what feelings or behavior triggers it?

WHY I WANT TO STOP

I am choosing to change this BECAUSE…

MY QUIT PLAN IS:

REPLACEMENT ACTION PLAN

What new actions can I take instead of resorting to this habit (walk, knit, dance, sing, phone a friend etc…write down your plan here.

## END SESSION

**Always end by tapping in the positive empowering reminder phrase:**

**"I choose to let this bad habit go...right now I am safe and whole to pursue my goal."**

## FUTURE SELF TAPPING

Look into the future and see your Future Self having succeeded in releasing bad damaging habits, including this one.

Attune with this Future Self...feel how they feel...see how they see the world with unshakable confidence and wellbeing, totally FREE of this habit.

# CHAP 6 BIGGEST BLOCK

## YOUR "BIGGEST BLOCK"

*I*f you repeatedly fail to come through on goal – it could be you have a deep inner conflict. Perhaps parts of yourself are pulling in different directions, each well-intentioned to protect you in some way.

## TESSA FEARED SUCCESS

An example is my client Tessa who finally realized her failure to expand on her business and projects was more a fear of SUCCESS than failure. Part of her feared that becoming too successful had certain drawbacks which she'd never admitted to yourself.

**Fear she might neglect her family, children and partner if she got "too busy".**

Pinpoint this potential fear of success - or any other constraint holding you back as follows:

Start slow tapping as you ask yourself...repeatedly... in a curious frame of mind:

*What is the single biggest block or constraint that is stopping me from achieving my goal?*

Sit quietly with a notebook/journal (you can use the My Tapping

Notes below) as you methodically and hypnotically tap your body, eyes closed for further insight, asking:

*What is the problem holding me back?*

*What else is the problem?*

Tap slowly, saying these statements in a curious frame of mind until specific answers pop up:

- The main reason stopping me is...
- I can't do this because...
- It's not possible for me to achieve this goal because...
- A part of me is resisting...I wonder why?
- Or maybe it's not really important...
- But maybe it is...so what's holding me back?
- What could I DO to break through or release this block?

# TAPPING NOTES

## THIS BIG BLOCK

**MY "BIGGEST BLOCK"**

Look for an inner conflict, past trauma or memory from the past or your Younger Self who shows up as you tap...a part of you that shows up as causing the block.

Write your insights here – and come back to it in the next few weeks to see what else comes up for you.

Commit to a Tapping Schedule to release, dissolve and overcome this block for goal success.


MY TAPPING SCHEDULE WILL BE:

Always end with the positive empowering reminder phrase as you tap:

**"I choose to let this go...right now I am safe and whole to pursue my goal."**

* * *

## END SESSION

**Always end by tapping in the positive empowering reminder phrase:**

**"I choose to let this block (name it) go...right now I am safe and whole to pursue my goal."**


## FUTURE SELF TAPPING

Look into the future and see yourself having succeeded in releasing your biggest block (which you were never consciously aware of).

Attune with this Future Self...feel how they feel...see how they see the world with unshakable confidence and wellbeing, totally in the flow of their dreams and goals and cheering you for having released the block at this time.

# CHAP 7 LOSING MOMENTUM

## EXPECT SET BACKS

*W*hat stops so many people from changing their lives is a seeming set-back that crushes their former intention and momentum.

They feel daunted by the sheer size of their chosen goal and so revert back to inertia.

It's so much easier to dream big but take no focused action in the hope that the Law of Attraction will magnetize it your way!

Expect set-backs and plan to keep going anyway.

Marcus Aurelius, the great Stoic **wrote**:

*"Our actions may be impeded, but there can be no impeding our intentions or dispositions*

Losing traction and motivation after a few weeks or months is a common occurrence but need not be a goal stopper for you.

*Do not let it impede your path or force you to give up on your goal.*

The question is how to avoid failure in the long-term and stay – or get back – on track?

## MAGIC OF MOMENTUM

Like goal guru Brian Tracy, **I recommend you do something every day that moves you toward your most important goal.**

Make a habit of getting up each morning, planning your day to do something, anything, that moves you at least one step closer to what is most important to you.

You will never lose momentum for long with **daily action steps** because it deepens your thought patterns, commitment and belief that the goal is achievable, thus activating the Law of Attraction with action.

## CHOOSE 3 THINGS

I suggest choosing 3 Things you plan to do each day, as opposed to a long TO DO List.

"If you have more than 3 priorities you don't have any," according to Jim Collins.

As a result, you begin moving faster and faster towards your goal and your goal moves faster and faster towards you.

**Achieving a goal becomes easier and faster with EFT Tapping to kick-start each day with a reminder to your brain and nervous system about your intentions and intended actions.**

# TAPPING NOTES

## KEEP MOMENTUM

Begin tapping while you remind yourself of the Stoic saying that "the obstacle is the way or path" to your greatest good and goals.

Look back on your past failures and successes with achieving important goals and makes notes about the OBSTACLES you encountered.

### TAP ON PAST FAILURES

Tap away the intensity of past failures - many are "goal traumas" you have buried and secretly blame yourself for failing to achieve.

    Name one here:

### TAP ON PAST SUCCESS

To balance the downside, look for the upside you can celebrate about your past successes.

    **3 Success goals I have achieved that make me proud:**

List below positive empowering affirmations you can use for Tapping to encourage you to be prepared to keep FOCUS and MOMENTUM, no matter what.

For instance start to implement the **3 Things Daily List**. And cheer your successes every day.

## END SESSION

**Always end by tapping in the positive empowering reminder phrase:**

**"I choose to let this block (name it) go…right now I am safe and whole to pursue my goal."**

## FUTURE SELF TAPPING

Look into the future and see yourself having persisted - no matter what the obstacles on in the way.

Attune with this Future Self…feel how they feel…see how they see the world with unshakable confidence and wellbeing, totally in the flow of their dreams and goals and encouraging you to let go and release the block now.

# CHAP 8 PROCRASTINATION

## DON'T PROCRASTINATE - PRODUCE AND FINISH

*E*ver felt like you were in a tug-of-war inside, pulled in two directions at the same time? You want to get started towards an important project or goal, but can't, don't or won't?

### INNER CONFLICT

When my clients get frustrated and wail they are procrastinating, I usually stop them in their tracks and help them spot the inner conflict and reframe their pain like this:

> *"How about recognizing that there is a part of you that absolutely wants to do it and a part of you that for some reason feels ambivalent, scared or resistant?"*

This comes as a huge relief because they can then address the part that is holding them back and so end the inner conflict.

It means they can start to see themselves as "**producers and not procrastinators**" in the words of top Matrix Reimprinting trainer Ted Wilmot.

And stop "polishing" as creativity genius and author Sark puts it:

*"If you are writing or creating anything new, it is easy to become trapped in some form of polishing. Polishing by itself isn't bad, what's not good is incessantly delaying a creation based on what one or more of your inner critics say about it."*

## HOW TO TACKLE THIS GOAL STOPPER

Begin by feeling the feeling fully in your body, while tapping and talking until a scene or memory from the past pops up. It may be recent or from any time in your life going back to childhood. Step into the memory and create rapport with the Younger Self who is pulling back or fearful, tapping lovingly and asking what is happening.

## TAP YOUR YOUNGER SELF

Help your Younger Self to move through the fears expressed, tapping on him or her as you do so. Gradually as he or she feels understood, supported and loved, he or she will reveal what needs to happen and what resources are required to take action.

Changing this (and many other related scenes and pictures in your field or matrix) changes your belief and self-image to that of **producer not procrastinator**. This will set up a new field for getting things done and confidently producing excellent results for goal success.

# TAPPING NOTES

## PROCRASTINATION

**Start Tapping in a CURIOUS way asking: What inner conflict might be causing me to Procrastinate?**

Ask that resisting part: "What are you afraid of?"

Do not be surprised if he/she is afraid firstly of failure and all it implies - but also succeeding and the compromises or sacrifices that come with that.

On a Scale of 1 – 10 how intense is the resistance you feel about starting/finishing your project?

Where in my body is it?

Does it have a shape, color or feel?

As you tap a full round ask:

**Does a past memory - person, place or emotion - come to mind while I tap on this Procrastinating Part?**

\* \* \*

## END SESSION

**Always end by tapping in the positive empowering reminder phrase:**

"I choose to let this block (name it) go...right now I am safe and whole to pursue my goal."

## FUTURE SELF TAPPING

Look into the future and see your Future Self as a doer, accomplishing her goals easily and effotlessly.

Attune with this **Future Self**...feel how they feel...see how they see the world with unshakable confidence and wellbeing, totally in the flow of their dreams and goals and encouraging you to face the Twin sisters of Procrastination and Perfectionism which often go hand in hand.

# CHAP 9 PERFECTIONISM

## PERFECTIONISM

## PERFECTIONISM

*P*erfectionists can NEVER WIN.

Perfectionism is having a rigid high standard for yourself which is almost unattainable. It manifests as striving to get it exactly right, firstly for you, but also to impress or please others. It goes hand in hand with procrastination. The two feed off each other.

I call them the Toxic Twin Sisters because they are joined at the hip.

Most of the time perfectionism stems from parental programming. But not always.

Perhaps your parents wanted to live vicariously through your achievements and so "encouraged" you with words like: "where is the other 2 %?" when you got 98% for an exam.

I'm the exception because my parents were unconditionally supportive but the German nuns at my Roman Catholic convent school imprinted two perfectionist tendencies that I have spent a lifetime bringing into balance:

• Strive to be "perfect" and without sin in the eyes of God
• Strive to excel and get close to perfect results academically

My perfectionism as a writer nearly caused me to have a nervous break down when after university I became a cub reporter in a news-room and had to write to a fast deadline.

To this day when I sit down to write a blog or book, I am aware of the ghosts of Perfectionism and Procrastination hovering in the near distance, waiting to swoop down and bring Resistance to me achieving my work.

Thank goodness I have EFT and Matrix Reimprinting to come to the rescue of any little ECHOs still imprinted with perfectionism.

I can step into the matrix, hear why and where they feel paralyzed or stuck, liberate them from the voices of perfectionism imprinted in memory – and give them (and the Adult me) inspiring and empow-ering resources and pictures to re-energize my current writing goals.

# TAPPING NOTES

## PERFECTIONISM

Look at a project you have been meaning to start or complete.

**Start Tapping in a CURIOUS way asking: What inner conflict might be causing me to feel I have to get it perfect?**

Ask that Perfectionist part: "What are you afraid of if it's not perfect going ahead with my goal?"

## NAME THE FEELINGS OR MEMORIES THAT COME UP.

On a Scale of 1 – 10 how intense is the feeling?
Where in my body is it?

Does it have a shape, color or feel?

## DO A ROUND OF TAPPING AND CHECK THE NEW LEVEL OF INTENSITY

Ask yourself: "Does a past memory - person, place or emotion - come to mind while I tap on this Perfectionist Part?"

\* \* \*

## END SESSION

**Always end by tapping in the positive empowering reminder phrase:**

"**I choose to let this block (name it) go...right now I am safe and whole to pursue my goal.**"

## FUTURE SELF TAPPING

Look into the future and see yourself having succeeded in **winning over your inner Perfectionist.**

Attune with this **Future Self** - feel how they feel...see how they see the world through eyes no longer sabotaged by perfectionism but able to flow freely in the directions of your dreams and goals and encouraging you to know you are perfect as you are.

# CHAP 10 OVERWHELM

## OVERWHELM

*S*o much to do and so little time!

Overwhelm guarantees you will lose sight of your dreams and goals.

But it doesn't have to be that way!

You know you're overwhelmed when you:

- Feel emotionally frazzled
- Have an impossible "To Do" list every day
- Set too many New Year resolutions or unresolved goals
- Can't say "no" or say "yes" out of guilt (both symptoms of people-pleasing)
- Have poor time management and organizational skills
- Can't make a simple decision about what to do next

## SOLUTIONS FOR OVERWHELM

Start with EFT Tapping.

Script for EFT Tapping for Overwhelm

Here's an example of an EFT Tapping script for OVERWHELM which starts out at a high intensity of 8-10.

## EFT TAPPING FOR OVERWHELM: SET UP PHRASES

Karate chop spot on either hand: tap as you repeat these phrases out loud, (or change the words to fit your exact situation):

"Even though I feel overwhelmed by my life, I choose to love and accept myself anyway."

"Even though I feel swamped by overwhelm, I deeply and completely love and support myself anyway."

"Even though I feel as if I'm drowning right now, I choose to love and support myself in this moment. I can breathe deeply and let go."

Top of Head: "I'm so behind with everything...it's all so overwhelming"

Inside Eyebrow: "All this overwhelm"

Side of Eye: "Drowning in things to do"

Under Eye: "Confused and overwhelmed"

Under Nose: "Should I do this...or that?"

Chin: "Frazzled and overwhelmed"

Collarbone: "Not sure what to think...or how to cope"

Under Arm: "So much to do...it's all too much"

Once you've reduced the intensity in the moment to a level of about 5 or less, it's time to find an ECHO in the past and proceed with a session of Matrix Reimprinting.

## YOUNGER YOU TRAUMA

Here you will discover and release specific past memories, beliefs and coping strategies from a Younger You. Start by dropping into the overwhelm feeling while you keep tapping.

Feel the feeling in your body and ask: "When have I felt like this before?"

You may go back to a specific memory – or even a situation with a person like your mother who seemed to be so overwhelmed that it affected you.

In my own case, feeling overwhelmed took me back to ECHOs

from my childhood, growing up with an alcoholic father. I often experienced home life as chaotic and overwhelming.

**My mother's overwhelm** in this situation definitely affected me deeply and gave me the belief that "life is overwhelming".

Thanks to EFT and Matrix Reimprinting I have cleared many of my own patterns and tendencies to feel overwhelmed and now help others to break free so they can do the same.

# TAPPING NOTES

## OVERWHELM

On a Scale of 1-10 how "Overwhelmed" and frazzled are you feeling?
    Remember to BREATHE and drink water as you go.

Where in my body is it?

Does it have a shape, color or feel?

### DO A ROUND OF TAPPING FOLLOWING THE EFT TAPPING SCRIPT

Tap until the feeling of overwhelm is lessened and forgive yourself for letting your life get to the point where you didn't say "No" to prevent this happening.
    Is there a person or situation contributing or causing the Overwhelm?
    Do you feel hopeless and helpless?
    Keep tapping.
    When you begin to feel calmer, make some notes about causes and the way forward to lessen the overwhelm.

\* \* \*

## END SESSION

**Always end by tapping in the positive empowering reminder phrase:**

"**I choose to let this block (name it) go...right now I am safe and whole to pursue my goal.**"

## FUTURE SELF TAPPING

Look into the future and see your Future Self smiling, cool and calm - handling life with confidence and ease.

Attune with this **Future Self** - feel how they feel...see how they see the world through eyes no longer frazzled and easily able to cope with life and people, easily and effortlessly.

# AFTERWORD

## THANKS

Thanks for your time and attention and I hope this book has enlightened and inspired you.

You need no longer feel alone or fearful when any of these 10 Goal Stoppers challenge your progress to live the life you love, setting and achieving your dreams and goals.

PLEASE WRITE A REVIEW IF YOU FELT THIS BOOK HELPED YOU IN ANY WAY AND WOULD LIKE TO RECOMMEND IT TO OTHERS.

**If you do - email or contact me below and I'd be happy to have a chat to help you get clarity about breaking -free of the goal-stoppers keeping *you* stuck.**

**EMAIL**: contactcwestmore@gmail.com

**INSTAGRAM:** @CarylWestmoreUK (Direct Message me)

**FACEBOOK**: Friend me and DM me: @CarylWestmore or @CarylWestmoreAuthor

I'll gladly help you to break-free on a ZOOM call.

Don't waste another minute of your precious life – BANISH, BAN

AND SAY BYE-BYE TO YOUR GOAL STOPPERS...so you can live the awesome, unstoppable, stupendous LIFE YOU LOVE!